A Floundering Quest for Love

OrangeBooks Publication

Website: www.orangebooks.in

First Edition 2025

Cover Design by Veeksha Vagmita

ISBN: 978-93-6554-720-7

Price: Rs. 250.00

Printed in India

A Floundering Quest for Love: Poems

VEEKSHA VAGMITA

OrangeBooks Publication
www.orangebooks.in

For all those men who broke me, helping me discover new layers, abilities and shades in myself. You transformed me.

Contents

Preface

Love is a subject that is at the heart of most poetry, and even after inspiring poems aplenty, it hasn't lost its irresistible pull. As a theme, it is a well-spring of possibilities enlivened by its sublime beauty. Though love is known to suffuse relationships with soul, sweetness, sacredness, sizzle, spark, and what not—all underpinned by steadfast devotion and a sturdy commitment—it is equally capable of engendering bitterness and profound sadness. In a happy scenario, it can be as smooth as a placid lake, but it carries within it the potential of turning into a raging river that can assault you with its violent waves. Love can be the catalyst for your awakening; it can also be your undoing. It can bring lasting joy or leave permanent scars. The poems in this collection look at the baffling complexities of love, entwined with longing and heartbreak. A cauldron of simmering emotions, love can be stirring, bruising, maddening, devastating and even life-

draining. ***Nothing hurts like love, and nothing haunts like its memories.***

The poems in this collection are on a theme—love, love, love—explored vastly, deeply and diversely over centuries, yet its appeal remains just the same and its charm simply refuses to wane. Love is one of those rare things that never stop giving, whether it is strength, delight or the inspiration to write.

I hope readers will find the poetry engaging and entertaining, absorbing and accessible. Crafted with great care, the poems should speak to the readers' hearts as much as to their intellect. Without any literary pretensions, this collection offers stimulating content and some delectable food for thought. The poems have been infused with thoughtful feelings and animated with emotionally rich thoughts.

This book is a love letter to bittersweet love.

The pieces of verse in this collection are witty, wild, wistful, wishful, and even fanciful, with several poems offering an inventive take on popular songs. The content and tenor of the poems is likely to elicit a gamut of responses: delight, laughter, sorrow, longing, desire, deep reflection, and the Aha! moment of resonance. The collection begins with a probing look at Miley Cyrus's song on self-empowerment ("I Can Buy Myself Flowers") and ends with Taylor Swift's lament on the murder of a love no less than a masterpiece. Some of the poems have emotional weight and are likely to provoke deep reflection. Other poems have a lightness to them—reading these verses should be a breeze and a delight. The book is supposed to be a happy combination of gravity and levity. Ultimately, this collection is about the volatility and intricacies of love, captured by unpretentious, penetrating verse.

Veeksha Vagmita

'I like not only to be loved, but also to be told that I am loved.'

— George Eliot

1

Should I Buy Myself Flowers? A Serious Question for Miley Cyrus

I have a serious question for Miley Cyrus

A question she certainly won't care to answer

The chasm between us is so enormous

That my voice would never reach her ears

I am an ordinary mortal stumbling through life,

while her fame has lit up the boundless sky.

Still, I will give it a try

and give voice to the quandary

preying on my mind.

I can buy myself flowers

The song just set me on fire

It was a seductive idea to be your own lover

Being solo never felt cooler

Yet, I couldn't help but wonder
What would I do with a present
that didn't qualify as a gift?
I may sound like a pedant
But flowers come to life
when they carry someone else's stamp
and are offered as a gesture of affection
by a Real Man.

So, it couldn't have made any bloody sense
to bombard myself with flowers
that a Sexy Nobody decided to send!

And yet, how liberating it was to buy
dainty blossoms that dazzled the eye—
A lovely gift from me, myself and I.

Who needed a knight in shining armour—
the modern version of that legendary figure—

to flaunt his gallantry with trite gestures?
How lazy it is to woo your lady love
with the fading appeal of flowers—
you can trust them to be as short-lived
as the lover's transient ardour.
The "knights" of today are as predictable
as their rehearsed flattery—
designed to break down your walls swiftly.
And when, with time, their passion wanes,
they break your heart just as easily.

When the allure of becoming empowered
by bringing myself hand-picked flowers
paled enough to help me see clear,
I cringed at the hitherto fancy notion
of pampering myself like a lover.
I would rather buy myself nothing
than create a self-consoling bubble.

I'm no princess who glories

in gifts bestowed liberally

Nor do I have a narcissistic propensity

to seek validation through bouquets

designed especially for me.

I am enough and I know it

But I don't need to show it

or induce envy in others

by displaying flowers

that declare the presence of an imaginary lover

as the scent of romance washes over visitors.

I could buy myself a flower shop

and yet feel lonely and adrift.

I could lie blissfully on a bed of roses

if the thorns wouldn't prick.

I could talk to myself for hours

But that won't fill the void within.

A gift for all times, flowers symbolize
the one thing missing glaringly from my life:
Love with radiance and a rosy fragrance.

The song was a roaring success
and richly deserved the plaudits
Oh, it is so damn infectious
The lyrics keep hovering over my lips.
I secretly bought myself flowers
But it failed to do the trick.
Their bloom mocked my loneliness
and were no match for the pure bliss
of knowing in your very bones
that you are loved by someone who really exists.

Hoping to discover the secret joys of being solo
I decorated my room with flowers of every hue
But their cloying scent gave me the blues
Killing me with the stinking truth

that even in my mid-thirties,

I have no adoring lover

who would find it worth his while

to buy me some goddamn flowers!

Man! I'm done with Miley Cyrus.

2

Not a Beautiful Disaster

So, you thought you could go on playing games?
You coveted my money while pushing me away!

So, you thought you could get away by asserting your brute power?
Did no one ever tell you that you can outdo a recalcitrant toddler?

So, you thought you could have your way by flaunting who you are?
Who are you anyway?

So, you thought you could never be dumped?
Sorry, you've not been in my heart for months.

So, you thought you could side with the devil while maintaining a façade of principles?

You belittle yourself by bootlicking your leader
Am I expected to applaud such behaviour?

Man, you turned out to be a complete loser!
Secretly wrapped around someone's fingers?
Oh, Jesus!

Nothing can conceal your screaming disloyalty
So, please spare me your perfunctory apologies.

Wake up and face the truth, my perfidious lover
Or, just leave it, I don't care any longer.

Anyway, good luck with your next partner
As for me, I feel so much lighter.

Man, this was such a disaster!

PS: The title of this poem is a nod to Kelly Clarkson's song "Beautiful Disaster".

3

Alone, Alone, Alone

How did it happen?

It was out of the blue

Living with her loneliness

She had forgotten the notion of "me and you"

Never had she imagined herself

A virgin in her thirties and still full of fire

Her youthful fantasies charged with desire

Had put her on a different route

The raging hormones threatened to spill over

Pestering her to shed her inhibitions forever

Thinking of it now, she prided herself

on choosing self-control

The desires that once made her toss and turn

Slowly waned as life went on

Till they troubled her no more.

Did it even happen?

Or was her imagination running wild?

The one made for her had finally materialised?

Heady with excitement, she felt out of her mind

The gods had sprung on her a splendid surprise

A hopeless romantic, a seeker of pure love

She had discussed with her potential lovers

books famed for portraying grand passion

Talked about the sublime beauty of true love

Hoping to set things in motion

And it worked really well

in the first flush of passion.

A tender love began to blossom

But wilted before it could reach fruition.

How she yearned for a partner day and night!

But the relationships, for all their sublimity,
never took flight!
Such was her wretched plight
that the one thing she had deeply desired
was just the thing she was constantly denied.
Famously solitary, she lost some of her pride
She stopped sharing her opinions
No longer could she take on the cynics
by asking the pointed question—
What was life without a companion?
Well, she herself had become a great example
of life without the pleasure of a union.

While all her friends found someone
that seem to fit them right
Love played with her wicked games
And life was truly unkind
Whenever she had wanted someone
with every piece of her heart,

It turned out to be no better than a mirage.

Relationships going strong simply fell apart

She had tried and tried

And finally given up.

Now, suddenly she had found real love

She wanted to believe it was no flight of fancy

Her heart said this was truly her destiny

She could not have been more wrong

And yet, she was perfectly right

But only if things were seen a particular light.

She was given to seeing the brighter side

even when red flags stared in the eye

That was the tragedy of her life.

She reciprocated the feelings

expressed secretly by the other side—

Feelings that were always kept under wraps

And never saw the day of light

Leaving her shattered inside.

Was her fierce criticism, her candid confessions,
responsible for her plight?
Did she scare men off
by looking reality in the eye?
by refusing to be content with a dreamland
removed from life?
by rejecting the waiting game and detecting
honey-dipped lies?
She couldn't be subservient
She could only be polite
She was willing to adjust and accommodate
But was always possessive of her space.

Though she loved with deep sincerity
She always came up empty.
That was the mystery
That was the quandary

She had stopped seeking answers
from the capricious universe.
She had stopped lamenting
the terrible twists her life had taken.
She had made peace with the quirks of fortune
and the absence of a companion
She didn't look for a reason
because life had its own rhythm
It was like a poem
with much that rhymed
and much that was random.
And that randomness admitted no explanation:
It was destiny
It was probability
It was fate
It was preordained.

Maybe the love that had held her captive

all of a sudden
was the poem that had been waiting
so long to be written.
This love had a force
that seemed strong enough
to kindle her dying hopes
and heal the parts that still hurt.

Distance posed a barrier
that bothered her too much
Love it was, maybe more than love
But it was devoid of the soothing touch
that she craved so much.
His expressions of love: pure and deep
Seemed so honest, they made her weep
But it was as if they were divided by a stream
He was close to her heart but out of her reach
His world was far removed from hers

Maybe the distance could never be bridged
But she wasn't the one to give up on a dream
Some cynicism would've saved her copious tears.

Defying all odds, she reached the other side
of the metaphorical stream—the great divide
Strangely enough, he was nowhere in sight
(She should have turned back right then
The realization came in retrospect
It was too late for course-correction
Though she had ample time for self-flagellation.)
She waited expectantly, willing to take a chance
He had evinced such eagerness even from afar.
His feelings had been strong
He should be there before long.
She waited for days in a kind of daze
Felt the thrill of anticipation
with the first stirrings of love

holding the promise of a lasting union.

She waited with trembling desire

She waited with her heart and soul on fire

She was on the edge of something sublime

She held out for a very long time.

This love may have seemed truly special

Still, it was no better than an illusion

Even if it carried the weight of great emotion.

Wiping her tears, she headed back home

She had come all alone

And was leaving all alone

She was alone

Alone.

4

'Since You've Been Gone': Musings on Kelly Clarkson's Musical Rage

As I saw the video of that anger-fuelled song
Questions crowded my law-abiding brain
Clarkson just exploded in rage
and pitilessly ravaged her lover's place.
I felt sorry for the guy
His pockets would be emptied
in getting his house back into shape.
He's probably not a celebrity
like Clarkson and her mates
No battery of attendants is at his beck and call
He would have to himself clear the trash and all
Nor can he refurbish his flat on a whim
He's not rolling in cash like Ms Clarkson.

I really can't make sense of the revenge

The guy was thankfully gone
and she could finally breathe again.
So, what made her smash voiceless objects
that gave no offence?
She could have gone her way
with graceful acceptance
What was the point of all the vandalism
and the glamorous show of vengeance?

I think they got the lyrics of the song all wrong
Kelly had no intention of moving on
She just wanted to ransack her lover's home
To give him a rude shock when he would return
A punishment for leaving her alone
It seems she never wanted him gone
No wonder, his absence made her go berserk.
When he would see the ruins of his possessions
He would certainly scream himself hoarse

And turn into the very image of woe.

Then Kelly would change her tune

And talk about starting anew:

I'll get us a luxurious home, don't you fret

This place was anyway too much of a mess

You're a moron, I can't help but confess

But I will stick with you nevertheless

'Cos my life will suck without you

But that's a different sound track

Sorry for the mix-up

and breaking a lot of stuff.

I'll have it fixed soon enough.

She had let out all her steam

Whatever she laid her hands on

was broken and torn to bits.

She waited for him to change his mind and come

Despite the wreck, he'd get a warm welcome

He didn't show up, though she waited for long
She began seething with anger once again
She left him a threatening voice message:
"You've been gone for way too long
Come back before I write another nasty song
Vandalise your property and have a ball
Is that what you want?"

The petrified lover emerged at last
One look at his house
and he ran back to his hideout
A luxurious refuge where he won't be found out
Now he lounges there with a sense of triumph
All that aggression couldn't keep him shackled
He listens coolly to Kelly's litany of woes
Set to admittedly catchy music
Dapper as ever, he's looking for a new chick
He's moved on from his volatile romance
With the furious, feisty Kelly Clarkson

He's truly and completely gone

And it doesn't merit another song.

Note: This is a fanciful take on the love-gone-sour depicted in Kelly Clarkson's famous song "Since U Been Gone".

5

Waiting

He picked up the phone

for the umpteenth time

Words lay heavy on his tongue

He pursed his lips to hold them in.

Those words had once flowed like wine

So heady, so exquisitely fine.

Now the sunny days

were engulfed by gloom.

Where love had blossomed,

weeds had grown.

Love's spring had come and gone

So transient, so lifelong.

Doubts lurked in his mind,

ravaging the garden of his life.

He missed the warmth of her smile

If only she had stayed a while.

The prayers, the tears—

love's lost labour.

The angst, the fever,

aggravated with the hours.

He dialled her number

with trembling fingers.

The ringing of the phone;

the pounding of his heart.

The buzzing in his ears;

the rawness of his nerves.

The warmth of her voice;

the breaking of the ice.

Weak at the knees,

he kept his manly poise.

The universe held its breath:

Will he dare? Will he dare?

Banish his sticky fears

Release the trapped words into the air

Let the unspoken finally have its say

But can he take on the universe

and dare to disturb its equilibrium?

Waiting, waiting

on the other side of the line

She can hear his uneven breathing

Almost feel his heart pounding

In sync with her throbbing desire

To hear "he's willing"—

A plain admission of his feelings

But all she hears is silence

loaded with words firmly held in

He is willing! Is he willing?

Waiting, waiting

Till the line disconnects

Not a single word was said.

Note: The poem is partly inspired by "The Love Song of J Alfred Prufrock", by T S Eliot. It also as an allusion to *David Copperfield*, by Charles Dickens.

6

The Love Laws

Part I

His words set off a melody in her heart

He had gained a rare mastery of his art

An orator like no other

He infused life into every theme

fetched from a brain: capacious and agile

It would leave his listeners mesmerised.

He painted with his words a panoramic view

with all the particulars, however minute.

This rendering of the minutiae

alongside the macrocosm

was jaw-dropping in its rigour and precision.

Every word that was chosen,

was chosen for a reason

So apt it was that it felt irreplaceable

Like the exact piece of a jigsaw puzzle.

As soon as he appeared, a huge crowd gathered

Drinking every word from his fount of wisdom

Their eyes glinted as they looked at each other

Wordlessly exalting the knowledgeable orator

No one knew his name or from where he came

He called himself a crusader

resolved to banish the darkness of ignorance

and eliminate the scourge of divisiveness.

He taught political science, philosophy,

sociology and literature with incredible ease

Interspersed with the lessons

were simple, organic sermons

Serving as a means

for the cultivation of people's conscience

Every utterance struck a deep chord

with his listeners

His solemn lectures often reduced them to tears.

When his lessons question settled assumptions

The hub of intellectual activity became a

battleground of ideologies

Ideas, beliefs and biases

warred for legitimacy and primacy.

Here she was attending another teaching session

with a furrowed brow and eyes wide open.

She wrestled with the people usurping space

to get a better view of the man

she liked to imagine as her flame

The one she'd marry and take on his name

She could easily meet the teacher's gaze

if only the morons would budge from their place.

She finally located a suitable spot

and experienced a strange thrill

Their eyes met instantly

Everything came to a standstill

For a few endless moments

They were transported to another realm

But the spell broke to resume the lessons

Her head spun with snatches of information

A semi-literate woman,

she couldn't win him with her intelligence

But she had a deadly weapon in her arsenal:

Her womanly charms and exceptional beauty

And that was no small advantage

She elbowed her way through the crowd

as a wispy plan turned rock-solid.

⁂

Who can resist the dewy charms of a maiden?

Wiping beads of sweat from her forehead,

she hurried to a beauty salon:

the place for reclaiming your natural elegance.

The ministering fingers of a beautician

massaged her face with exotic creams

and unguents

while plucking out everything in excess.

Her bun was becoming loose

and the strands of stray hair fell over her eyes,

obscuring her vision

She needed nimble fingers

to style her hair with perfection

The push and pull of the rapturous audience

had crumpled her twice-ironed saree

Mortified by her unkempt appearance,

she took off the shabby garment

Signalling to the attendant

to display their collection in all its finery

Soon enough, a wide range of sarees

were displayed for her benefit

Their shimmer, fine texture, embroidery

and artistic splashes of colour

left her wondering which one to favour

over its equally dazzling "peers".

She chose the saree with a riveting peacock

design, sequined texture, a dark blue border—

the entire ensemble a medley

of aesthetically muted colours.

A plunging blouse, perfectly classy,

accentuated the fullness of her figure

Blouses had to be hooked in the front,

but this was a sartorial adventure

Matching earrings and a lovely necklace

were added for good measure

Though nothing was of high quality,

it was styled gracefully

Every inch of her saree, every single ornament,

was far from tawdry

She wore the saree swiftly,

forming the pleats with ease,

setting her pallu in a manner

that suggested both modesty and mischief.

Her hair was fashioned into something chic

A braided crown, a hairstyle made for her,

lent her the aura of a queen.

The facial and the threading

had been ticked off the list

It was time for the make-up with light touches

She was too pretty

to be liberally painted and powdered.

A light pink lipstick, a hint of an eyeliner,

a few brushstrokes of powder

and a dainty bindi on her forehead

gave her the allure of a show-stopper.

By the time she emerged

in all her sensual splendour,

the crowd was thinning

and the teacher's eyes were darting

from one woman's face to another.

Could it be that he had noticed her

and was longing for an introduction?

Suddenly, the teacher looked in her direction,

making her feel she would melt away

if he didn't remove his gaze.

He stared at her with abandon

while others giggled in amusement.

Though they expressed their ardour

with their smitten look

An experience for which many would die

The grand passion didn't stand a chance

In a world ruled by the Love Laws

Their love would never gain acceptance

They dreamed of meeting on the other side

Once delivered from their agonising lives

Or colliding once again in another lifetime.

The Love Laws strike at the root of our being

Alienating us from our true feelings.

Committed to his mission,

the teacher found distractions

But the young woman inched towards her grave

Her heart was smashed,

and she seemed to dwindle away,

She wandered with a wild look in her eyes

"For one glimpse of my beloved,

I will offer up my life."

Weakened by her unbearable suffering

She felt her end was nearing

In her final days, she longed to be reborn

To be given a fair chance to live like everyone

She waited patiently for death to come

Her tears had dried

and her hopes had evaporated

The wait ended sooner than expected

Relief came without undue delay

Bringing deliverance from all the pain

While she slept, oblivious to worldly cares

Her life slowly ebbed away.

Part II (in the form of a prose poem)

AFTER THE END

She was laid out on a white sheet with flowers scattered and her face mostly covered. Whenever someone lifted the cover for a brief glimpse, they were greeted by a perfectly serene face, exuding dignity even in death. Her brow had not a single wrinkle and a pale smile suggested a graceful acceptance of the inevitable. She was cremated honourably. The townsfolk had a rude awakening; their sunshine was replaced by a dark cloud with no silver lining. They decided to send an emotional note to their heartbroken teacher. This is what was written on a paper stained with tears:

When you are in love, you are in love. It is what it is, and there's nothing that can be done. An irrepressible force, love crosses all social boundaries. It is the greatest challenge to a feudal, patriarchal society. We've had our days of passionate orthodoxy. They now seem like a parody of real sensibility. Thankfully, we've mellowed and matured with time. And yet, we'll be haunted by remorse all our lives. **That epitome of beauty—a distinct creation like you and me—suffered terribly for the presumed sin of falling in love with a man socially superior but equally besotted with her. These Love Laws are the bane of this world.** How we wish we hadn't fallen for such nonsense! You had warned us but we paid no heed. It is heart-breaking that a beautiful soul had to die for us to understand something that was no rocket science. It was just a reinforcement of our common humanity that dismantles all evil hierarchies.

Note: In The God of Small Things, Arundhati Roy talks about the Love Laws that decide who should love whom and how and how much.

7

'I Don't Know Why I Cry': Neither do I, Gwen Stefani

I didn't know you had the power
to make me sad again
That could've happened in a different lifetime
And this is a different epoch of my life
where you matter, but only up to a point.
And my feelings for you are too tepid
to let you move me like you once did.

But even now you managed to leave me bruised
with your rough-hewn, jagged words.
You touched and tore my rawest nerve
It's so like you to be so brusque
Not caring a fig how much it would hurt.

I don't I know why I cry silently

When I had conquered my vulnerabilities

I can't do better than Gwen Stefani

So, I'll just rephrase her eloquent rant—

I remembered suddenly

that a time there was in my life's history

when I used to love you like crazy.

But then I grew strong enough

to stand my ground.

You couldn't bully me as was your wont

You had hurt me enough over the years

And our undeclared romance was finally over

I carried so much pain deep inside—

the pain I had suppressed and denied.

Now I was ready for a jolly good fight

All my tender feelings had been left far behind

So, I don't know why I'm teary-eyed tonight.

Maybe I grew weak and remembered in vain
That things were so different back then
My passion was real and deeply sincere
But love's labour simply went down the drain.
As time passed and love's haze cleared
I grew resentful and put you in your place
I vowed to never let you dominate
Never again.

I wasn't going to wear my heart on my sleeve
I wasn't going to collapse on the bed and weep
I had to carry my sorrow like a dignified woman
I taught myself not to lose my self-possession.
Why do I cry then? I wonder once again
Gwen Stefani would understand in an instant
this concoction of perplexity and pain.

Oh yes, I know at last
What cut me to the bone—

He pushed me too far

With his angry tone

He needed a trash can for his messy emotions

And he dumped them on a person already broken

He had no qualms about being harsh

He just pushed me way too far

And so, I can't help but wonder

Why do I cry in the depths of my heart?

The answer is there in the arresting sound track—

Because there was a time in the past
when I used to love him
I used to *love* him
I used to love *him*
I'm not that "I" anymore
Then why do I cry for a guy I no longer adore?
If truth be told, I really don't know.

Note: This piece of verse was inspired by "Used to love you", a song, charged with raw emotions, by Gwen Stefani. The singer conveys a staggering range of emotions with subtle and powerful facial communication. Her expressive countenance is a poem in itself.

8

Change

I feel Change cruising towards me

Much deferred but still so sweet

The wait has ripened the fruit

of a love that strove to be freed.

The door of the cage is now open

Out flies the trapped bird.

Will Change heal my broken heart?

Or inspire some new work of art?

Would it work its magic by stealth?

Or land right at my doorstep?

Would my parched tongue find the words

to express a longing long suppressed?

Will Change come on Santa's sleigh

and answer my unheard prayers?

9

The Mysterious Ways of Love

The first time our paths crossed

I don't know how but I knew

That the bond we were still to forge

was bound to endure.

It was an inkling so slight

that I didn't even realise

when it rose to the surface

and barely left a trace.

Something tugged at my insides

But it didn't give me pause

So, it took me by surprise

when that fleeting emotion

that had signified so little

resurfaced with such a force

that I was almost at a loss for words.

What had just been an intuition

Too vague for recollection

Completely forgotten

Turned out to be the harbinger

of a memorable connection.

With or without words,

our relationship took shape.

Every time I think of it,

it leaves me amazed.

Our lives got entwined by an invisible thread

in ways I could never have dreamt.

But there are days when I'm gripped by dread

when forces too hard for us to withstand

leave us at our wits' end.

So, I thank the stars for keeping us together

Allowing our bond to grow stronger

I can't believe the storms we have weathered

without letting our devotion waver.

From the tip of your fingers

to the core of your being,

you have tried to stay true to me.

We've come so incredibly close

that every time I feel your presence

my love for you threatens to overflow.

Regardless of the seasons

and the vagaries of the weather

You were always and forever

a fervent well-wisher

and so much more …

10

All Too Well (in the Depths of Hell): Found a Kindred Spirit in Taylor Swift

If it makes you feel better,

I won't play the track over and over

That 10-minute bewitching ballad

by a Taylor less than swift

Brings to surface the pain that got repressed

Seeking expression through tears I haven't wept

The subtle agony in the strains of the music

Grows on you really quick

A fairly simple song can have its own magic

The slow build-up to the ultimate question

must feel like a pinprick

But the question must be asked, so ask I will:

My shadowy lover, have you found deep bliss?

Or were you maimed by the game

that stabbed my very soul?

Can you now ever be guiltless,

exuberant and whole?

Do the probing, haunting lyrics

move you with their yearnings?

A song written with supreme finesse

A masterpiece too modest to boast its brilliance.

What a fitting tribute to the rare camaraderie

that was torn up with careless ease

Now it all comes back like a frightening dream

of a romance butchered by you, **not me.**

Why do you keep my scarf if I was a Nobody

You know I was there, faithfully waiting

You know it like your breath

You know it all too well.

By now your illusions must have been dispelled

I hope you will finally admit

that you created a legendary mess

It could have been you and me

It could have been you

And it could have been me

It could have been anything

other than the madness you unleashed.

Have you faced that reality

after all these years?

Is your self-effacing charm

still masking your conceit?

When you think of your treachery,

your unforgivable deceit,

do you feel sorry for inflicting needless injuries?

Have you ever tried to imagine

the extent of my pain

that still flows like acid through my veins?

Do you remember the dream that you just let go?

But that was long ago.

And yet after all these years, I have a question for you

Why did you keep me lingering on the edge of hope?

Engulfed by loneliness, I watched your gleeful betrayal

You pushed me to the brink as if it was all a game

Does the fallout of your cheerful idiocy stare you in the face?

How casually you wrecked me with your cunning ways!

I wouldn't be sorry to see you suffer

You heard that right, my dear

I wouldn't care for your tears

Even Christ would lambast you for your sins

Some things can never be forgiven.

There was a time when I ached for you to give me closure

Now I would rather die than let you come closer

Your conscience was benumbed long ago

How you threw all scruples to the winds!

Just to protect your big, fat ego

Lying, lying, lying—

As if your life depended on it

I kept my promise to stay discreet

only to be rewarded with ridicule

And the credit for this goes entirely to you

It's no surprise that you were spineless

and untrue

After all, you can only be you.

Whether it was my idealism or innocent hopes,

I don't really know.

Just like that, I was made the butt of jokes

And ripped to shreds

While you pretended to be helpless

All those silly parties

resembling late-night shows

Only amplified your stupidity

with compliments galore

Spare me your apologies

and forget about reconciliation

A wayward freak, you are beyond redemption

No amount of your "love"

can ever give joy to anyone

I could have given my life for you

But you didn't even act human.

With abandon, you wrecked a blooming garden

I cried to see the ruins of myself

There's no doubt you will land up in hell

These memories will chase you all your life

I know you know it all too well.

Note: "All Too Well", by Taylor Swift, was the inspiration for this poem. A song with hidden depths, it can transport you to a different realm.